So You Want to Be a Cowboy?

by

Pat Puckett

ISBN-13: 978-1475076240

ISBN-10: 147507624X

I'd like to dedicate this book to my protégé's, Britani Cook and Jeff Kadansky.

From left: Jeff Kadansky, Pat Puckett, & Britani Cook (Courtesy of Tanya Hiple)

"If you'll get around the outside, the middle will take care of itself."

~ Ray Hammond, cow boss, Little Horn Ranch, Wyola MT

Part 1

Ridin' Job on a Northern Range Cow/Calf Operation

To work as a cowboy, you have to understand geography. Where you are geographically dictates what your job requires of you. The Northern Range encompasses eastern Washington, northern Idaho, Montana, and Wyoming. It is its own world.

The good news is the Northern Range is big, wide-open country with good grass and water. The bad news is the weather is tough for about 6 months out of every year, as in below 0° for many days in a row.

In this book, I'm going to talk about riding jobs on the bigger ranches that still run separate crews. There is typically a cowboy crew and a farm crew, mechanics, and seasonal irrigators. Most outfits with 2000 cows would have two full-time cowboys.

The actual dates I use in this book may be adjusted according to the elevation of different ranches but the big picture is what we're after.

The day to day work on a cow outfit is dictated by the date you turn the bulls in with the cows. The gestation period of a cow is 9 ½ months so if you turn the bulls in on June 1st, you'll start calving on March 15th. If you remove the bulls on August 1st (which means the job is complete by the 15th), you will have a 75 day breeding season. A cow comes in heat every 22 days so a 75-day breed up means she will have had three chances to conceive. Let's walk through the calendar.

January-February

It's January and the cows are going in to their third trimester. The temperature is below 0°. At this time of year, the cow herd is close to headquarters so they can be fed hay. The cattle might be in as many as 4 to 5 different pastures depending on water, protection from the elements, and proximity to hay storage. Two pastures will have the main cow herd, around 850 head per pasture. Another pasture would be your poor doers. Another pasture would be replacement heifers.

Every day the cows come to the feed ground to eat. You time it so you get to the feed ground before the feeding crew arrives. This gives you the opportunity to watch the cows as they walk in. Here are a couple of the many things to watch for: You might spot a cripple so you ride over and check it out. If it's a front foot, it could be a condition caused by a cow cutting a heel bulb on sharp ice when she goes to water at a creek. It's called "ice foot." Typically, you and your partner will rope her and doctor her by pouring a 7% iodine solution on the cut. Iodine will disinfect the wound and harden the skin. At 0°, flies aren't a problem.

When the cows are all strung out eating hay, you can ride past them and check their condition. Before they fill up on hay, you'll be able to see that they are bigger on the right side. This is where the calf lays inside the cow. You might see some that look suspiciously empty which means one of two things: she might be carrying her calf high so it will not show or she might have aborted her calf. When abortion occurs in the third trimester, it could be an indicator of disease.

After you look the cattle over, you'll ride the pasture to see if any cattle didn't go to the feed ground and investigate why that might be.

One of your jobs is to sort off the cows that aren't doing well so you can give them extra hay and protection from the wind. You'll put them in a pasture with natural cover like brush, trees, or willows.

This routine will go on through February.

One of the biggest problems with the Northern Range is that cattle have to be kept in close proximity all winter in order to be fed. This translates in to more health problems than you see in cattle that are spread out over thousands of acres. The trade-off is higher weaning weights than in other parts of the country.

Replacement heifers are pregnant females that will be having their first calf. Their winter ration is critical to their production. If a heifer is too thin, she won't be able to support her calf. If she's too fat, she will have trouble calving. On a 2000 head outfit, there will be around 200 replacements. Each year, the ranch will try to keep 10% of its heifer calves for replacements.

A rule of thumb for feeding cows is that you feed approximately 3% of a cow's body weight. When the temperature drops below 0°, you feed more.

Each day, you pick where you will start according to the priorities you have set. By now, you've figured out that you have to think on your own. Everyone else is just as busy as you are and the ranch is counting on you to get going and pay attention. Lazy people and drunks don't work out on ranches.

March

Calving Season

Calving season is the most stressful season on a ranch. Every person on the ranch is affected, from the cook to the mechanic. What happens during calving season dictates what happens when you sell the calves in the Fall.

The ranch only gets one paycheck each year. If you have a successful calving season and a good summer, you will sell 1800 calves in the fall. At $500 per head, the paycheck is $900,000. Remember, a cow only has one calf each year and every time a calf dies, it costs the ranch $500. As a cowboy, these are just two of the incentives you have to do the best job you can. An even heavier responsibility is the fact that you turned the bulls in with the cows so you are accountable for the well-being of every single cow.

During calving season, the cowboy crew increases from 2 to 6. You ride through the cows twice a day. The bigger crew stays on until the calves are branded and the cattle are on their summer pasture which is generally in June.

Calving means paying close attention to detail. Here's one scenario: You spot a cow off by herself about a half mile away. So you put her in your memory bank and make her part of your circle. As you approach her, you'll stay about 100 feet away and size up the situation. Determine if she has a kink in her tail, if she has broken water, or if she has a front foot showing. This will tell you how much time she has before she calves. You ride on and finish your circle. On the way back, you will ride back by the cow to check on her progress.

After a cow breaks water, she can calve anywhere from 10 minutes to 2 hours. After 2 hours, you have to make a decision about whether or not she needs help.

Heifers calve earlier than the cow herd because they are more labor intensive. It also takes them longer to recover after they calve. A cow can come in to heat 45 days after calving while a heifer can take as long as 60 days.

Calving heifers is the true test of a cowboy's skills. You have to make life and death decisions and you have to think for the heifer. Once the heifer breaks water, you're entered until the calf sucks and the heifer falls in love with it. Everything that can go wrong, does.

One of the nightmare situations happens when one heifer calves but another heifer, who is about to calve, claims the calf and lets it suck. Then the heifer who claimed the calf lays down and calves.

Now you have a wreck! You have to bring them all to the barn and parley them around until they pair up. This can take up a lot of valuable time. But it's just one of those things that happens and has to be addressed. I could write a whole book on calving. Maybe I will.

May

There are a lot of things going on all at once at this time of the year. You have a large number of cattle that need to get to summer pasture. The farmers want to prepare the hay meadows where the cows spent the winter. And of course you're going to get one more big snow storm just to keep you humble. Depending on the weather, spring works can take 3 to 8 weeks. In the Northern Range, everybody works for a woman – Mother Nature.

When I write about branding, remember this is from a cowboy's perspective. Usually the neighbors come over and you all gather around 300 pairs. When you get to the corrals, the cows are cut off and the calves are put in a branding corral. About 50 head are cut in to a smaller corral so they can be heeled and drug to the fire. Everybody who wants to rope is given a chance.

The boss will usually put a couple of good ropers in with a couple of beginners. This is how the kids learn the trade. After a long winter, branding is a social event with a lot of good food and visiting with neighbors and friends.

Before the cattle are turned back out, the "drys" (cows that didn't calve) are cut out. Dry cows are a liability and not an asset to the ranch. They will be sold when the market dictates. Everywhere you go, branding is handled a little differently. The end result is to have a return address stamped on each calf.

June-July

"Turning out" means trailing the cattle to their summer pasture. This is usually a forest permit, state land, B.L.M., or private leases. Typically you have a specific date that you are allowed to turn out and a specific date the cattle have to be off the permit land.

June is also when the bulls are turned out. Turning out bulls sounds simple but it can be dangerous business. I have seen a bull push another bull into a horse and rider, knocking the horse down. The result was a crippled horse and a crippled cowboy. The bottom line is that everybody on the crew needs to be on their toes.

Summer grazing is the highlight of the year. If you're lucky enough to spend the summer in a cow camp, you get paid off for all the hard work it took to get the cattle to their summer range. A camp man is responsible for keeping the cattle on the allotment and not letting them trash the areas around the water. He has to scatter bulls, check line fences, and doctor cattle.

My favorite job is packing salt. If you're packing two horses, you'll have 10 blocks of salt. This chore makes you slow down and leave camp at a walk. On most days, you're in a big hurry because you have a long way to go. But not when you're packing salt. If you use cowboy logic, packing salt is like a day off. It's the same thing as feeding with a team on a nice day. It doesn't matter that you had to buck bales!

August-September

You start gathering bulls on the 1st of August. This is a whole different ballgame than when you turned them out. Now it's hot and the bulls are brushed up. You are attempting to bring in an animal that weighs twice as much as you and your horse and he doesn't want to go anywhere.

The ratio of cows to bulls is 25 to 1. If you have 2000 cows, you are looking for 80 bulls plus the stupid bulls that belong to the neighbor that got in on you. By the way, the neighbor is saying the same thing about your bulls that got in on him! The last 20 are usually the ones that you really have to earn. All over the west, there are amazing stories about how the bulls were gathered.

After this chore is done, anybody who is due a vacation gets to take one.

September-October

The Round Up

Gathering in the fall means cleaning your country. You've been riding on your cattle all summer so you have a good idea where everything is. Since you just got done gathering bulls, you would have brought some cows in with them to get everybody closer.

I'm sure you've noticed by now that the things you do on a given day can affect your whole year.

Like everything else, there are many ways to do a round-up. I'll just give you one example. Most outfits have a trap which can be used to hold the cattle as you bring them in. The trap has not been grazed so there is plenty of grass. As the crew gathers the cattle from a given area of the summer range, they throw them in to the trap. Before you start trailing the cattle from the trap back to headquarters, you ride through them, doctor anything that needs it, and sort off the strays. Once this is done, you throw the gate and head for home.

October – November

Once you get back to headquarters with the cows, things get really busy. Hang in there with me. You'll get a day off "When the Work's All Done This Fall." For you youngsters, that's an old classic cowboy song. After reading this, you can appreciate the title.

The bulls need to be culled and located. When I say "located," it doesn't mean I don't know where the bulls are. The term "locating cattle" means to settle them in a pasture and put them on water.

The cows and calves need to be worked. Once again, every outfit has its own way of doing things. Here's one of those ways: If you have two weeks until the trucks arrive, you have two weeks to replace the weight they lost trailing home. The crew now consists of 10 cowboys. Part of the crew will be responsible for processing and the rest are shipping.

The crew rides out and starts working off pairs. What they are looking for are cows with high quality heifer calves that can be held for replacements. This would be around 225 head. You cut a few extra because by spring you'll have some you don't want. At the same time, they cut out cows with calves that are pottys which is a term for an inferior calf. These cows will be culled.

After working the herd, the cattle you cut off can be processed before you bring in the big bunch. "Processed" means weaning and vaccinating the calves. The cows are preg tested and the pregnant ones are vaccinated. The open and cull cows are put in a separate pasture and will be shipped with the culls from the main herd.

When you show up at the corrals on shipping day, you don't want to waste time or money.

Shipping day is the most important time of the year. The way the cattle are handled can cause the ranch to make or lose thousands of dollars in a single day. I'll share with you the simple math: On the day you ship, the calves are going to lose weight because you have to handle them in corrals and the close proximity causes stress. If a calf loses 5% of its 500 pound body weight, that is 25 pounds. At $1.50 per pound, that loss is $37.50. If you multiply that number by 1700 calves, you have lost $63,750. Now if you ship like a professional and the shrink is only 3%, each calf loses just 15 pounds which is $22.50. For 1700 calves, you will have lost $38,250. That's a difference of $25,500 which probably represents one cowboy's wages for the year.

It will take you two days to ship 1700 head of weaned calves. The herd will have been cut in half prior to shipping day. The crew walks the first half to the corrals. You will be set up to cut off the cows from the calves and then sort the heifer calves from the steer calves. Then you weigh the calves, steer calves first. When the calves come off the scale, they are loaded on to the trucks. Other than the crew on horseback, you have a brand inspector, a vet, the cattle buyer, and the boss running the scales.

By noon, the trucks are gone and everybody can take a breath.

Next, 200 more cows will be put in the corrals off feed and out of the way to be processed the following day.

The next day arrives none too soon and the last half of the herd is brought in. The same shipping program as the day before will take place again.

Meanwhile, the processing crew will deal with the 200 cows that were brought in the previous day. The cows will be preg tested, culled, and vaccinated. Two hundred head is a typical number that can be worked in a day. So you have to rotate cattle and feed until every cow has been worked. This will take about 10 days.

Now you can take a day off!

November ~ December

The crew goes back to just two cowboys. The ranch is getting quiet and other than riding on the pottys and the replacement heifers, checking the bulls and cows, you start getting ready for winter. Looking back on the last year, I think you can appreciate why it is called a "ridin' job."

During this whole story, you may have noticed that I never elaborated on the horse. A man on a horse cannot be replaced by a 4-wheeler or a closed-cab tractor or a pick-up. I know that all ranches have equipment to do the job. The point I want to make is that humans have become disconnected from the land and cattle because of machines. A man on a horse stays connected to the full meaning of working on a ranch. He is a true steward of the land and livestock under his care and has preserved a level of compassion that other parts of the "livestock industry" are lacking.

Part II

Ridin' Job on a Yearling Outfit

Let's take a look at what a yearling outfit is all about.

I've heard this type of operation called by many names such as steer outfit, stockers, grass cattle, and feeder cattle. It depends on what part of the country you're in. Many outfits are diverse which means they run both cow/calf and yearlings.

The difference between a cow outfit and a yearling outfit is this: When you run cows, you own the factory (the cow) whereas when you run yearlings, you have to buy them every year.

A yearling is a calf that has been weaned, is about 8 months old, and weighs around 500 pounds. The idea is to run this calf, which has either been raised on the place or purchased from somewhere else, when the grass is coming on. The grass season in the north runs from May through October. In most of California, it's from November through May.

Once again, Mother Nature is who we work for and water is the limiting factor. The availability of forage and the quality tells you what you can run on a particular ranch. The rule of thumb is 1 cow equals 2.5 yearlings. But it's more complicated than that.

I worked on a ranch in Nevada that had winter country and summer country. The forage consisted of summer grass and browse. It was 500,000 acres that ranged in elevation from 4000 feet to 9000 feet. We fed no hay. That situation made it a good cow outfit. Because of the terrain, elevation and low ADG (Average Daily Gain), it didn't work for yearlings. Central California, on the other hand, gets winter rains and is low elevation. You'll see the ranches there load up with yearlings every fall.

The object of a yearling outfit is to keep the cattle healthy and gaining weight. Depending on the year, the quality of the feed can drop quickly and the rate of gain on the cattle will take a hit.

Buying yearlings and making a profit in an eight month timeframe is not easy. You have to get up, get going, and pay attention.

For years, it worked well to buy light steers from Mexico. Now the states in Mexico that raise the best cattle have droughted out. Add to the equation the drug cartels and high trucking costs and you get a lower quality of steer that has to come from farther south.

The cattle market used to be dictated by the price of corn. Now we deal with a world market and weather. Everyone has an opinion so here's mine. The highest return available on a yearling outfit would be with heifers, not steers. Because of beef demand and drought, the female numbers are down. The timeframe between weaning and breeding a heifer can be filled on a yearling outfit. This idea can be implemented several different ways. Whoever is the most creative and has the sharpest pencil wins!

So let's get to work. If the ranch buys calves in October, they need to be processed when you receive them. This can involve vaccinating, worming, ear tags (not recommended), and branding. Processing 300 head per day is common. The distance the calves travelled and the condition they are in when they arrive dictates when you process. Some outfits let them rest on feed in a trap while others process right off the truck.

As the yearlings are worked, they are turned out in small traps prior to being turned out to pasture. There might be some that are too sick to turn out. For example, Mexican steers have to be dipped in a solution prior to crossing in to the U.S. They are completely submerged in chemicals to kill any bugs they might be carrying. Some swallow too much of this solution or inhale it into their lungs. By the time they get to the ranch, they're sick. All the good bacteria in their gut has been killed. They need to be drenched and watched closely. The good news is Mexican cattle are tough. If you're lucky, the sick ones are a little older than normal. I've seen a lot of long tails that are a year old and weigh 400 pounds.

They seem to come out better than the young ones.

Once you've turned out, you need to camp on 'em. About two weeks after processing, you'll notice most of your sickness shows up. As a cowboy, no matter how many thousand you've received, you have to treat the last one with the same regard as the first one. This is one of the biggest challenges.

Facts to ponder: NINETY PERCENT of death loss occurs in the first month of turn out and a dead steer shows no profit.

Each cowboy usually has his designated country to ride on. At first, you'll spend a lot of time locating the cattle on water and feed and getting them settled. They don't know the country and tend to walk the walls which means they head to the nearest fence and walk until they hit a corner then they turn and walk some more until they hit another corner and so on. You might find a hundred head stuck up on a brushy hillside acting like they can't get out. So you get them pointed the right direction and try to put them on water. This little chore might take you all day.

I've heard this same statement on every outfit I've worked on: "These are the dumbest SOB's I've ever seen!" If you're interested, those "SOB's" will teach you how to be in the right place and they will teach you patience. If you don't have any patience and aren't interested in learning anything, you'll never make a good hand.

As a cowboy, you're always on the lookout for sick cattle, inventorying your grass, checking water, keeping mineral and salt available, and when you're bored to death, riding fence.

When it comes to feed, a good practice is to test your grass for TDN (Total Digestible Nutrients) and protein at the beginning, middle, and end of the grazing season. You need to pay attention to the timing of washy grass, hard grass, and dry grass, from the back of your horse. The grass comes on all at the same time on many low elevation ranches. On broken elevation ranches, the grass comes on at different times so you can move the cattle with this cycle. The latter scenario gives you higher ADG because the cattle can be on the best feed with the highest value over a longer period of time.

As always, water is the limiting factor. Deferred, rotational, and intensive grazing are all good options for ranch management but you need to do your homework. To explain, if you're going to put a large number of cattle in a small area, you need to make sure there is plenty of drinking water for them. There is nothing worse than to ride up on 200 head of steers waiting on an 8-foot water trough to fill up that is running at a gallon a minute. Always remember, if you're burning more energy than you're producing, you are going backwards!

Sickness in cattle typically runs in cycles. You can start off with shipping fever which might be followed by pneumonia. Spotting sickness, like acute pneumonia, can be tricky. A steer might cough one time while it's walking along and that will be your only clue. As you watch closer, you might see a little drool coming out of its mouth, its head might be down, or it might just look a little weak. If you think it's sick, it probably is.

If you find a yearling laying down by itself at 8:00 in the morning, watch it. When it gets up, if it doesn't stretch, that's a clue. If it doesn't lick its nose, that's a clue. If it has a hump in its back, that's a clue. Once it's up, watch it walk. It might cough (pneumonia). It might gap at the mouth, have froth coming out of its mouth, and have a fast respiratory rate (shipping fever or anaplasmosis). If it's limping along, it might have foot rot. Walk along behind it and see if there's swelling between its toes. If it walks with its head cocked to one side, its ears could be full of ticks. Or it could have pink eye. These are just a few of the problems to watch for. All of them cause weight loss and can cause death.

Learn your cattle and learn their habits. You'll notice that healthy cattle won't be lying down at 8:00 in the morning and they're rarely by themselves. They should be grazing. Cattle are ruminants. They'll generally lie down when they're full and chew their cud.

You need to know what to do in many different situations. You need to have the skills to rope a sick animal, tie it down, and doctor it with the least amount of stress. There are lots of ways to doctor cattle. The circumstances you are faced with dictate how you go about it. The horse you're sitting on dictates how well you do it. That alone is the incentive to be a good horseman. A whole lot of good horses have been made on yearling outfits.

Another common problem in steer outfits throughout the west is that yearlings have a way of disappearing. Mexican steers are experts at hiding. Every cowboy has a story about a Mexican steer that laid down in the brush and wouldn't come out until the cowboy literally walked up to him and kicked him in the butt! "The longer the ear, the sneakier the steer."

If you're neighbor runs cows, you can count on finding some steer that has fallen in love with the cows. The process of getting this steer out can sometimes be a real contest. If possible, one of the best solutions is to load him up and relocate him to the opposite end of your country.

I once lost 9 head of Mexican steers right off the bat after I turned out. It took me three months to get them all back. I would find them hiding out in groups of 2 or 3.

When it comes to finding cattle, you need a really good horse that will go anywhere (a rock crusher) and a really good dog. Not a good dog, a really good dog. You, your horse, and your dog need to look for, listen for, and smell cattle. You also need to be good at reading sign. Above all, you have to be just a little bit smarter than a steer. That's the deal breaker.

At the end of the season, all your hard work is paid off when you hit the scales. Remember Mother Nature deals the cards. You have to play the hand you're dealt.

Part III

The Grazing Cell

When it comes to putting weight on cattle, there is another option: A grazing cell is a grass management system that optimizes the growth and value of feed. This program works the best in the southeastern U.S. The mild climate and abundant water compliments this type of grazing. It can be done in the west but you need the right ingredients to make it profitable.

I'm going to talk about one such example that had all the right ingredients in Wyoming. I set up a grazing cell on a 100-acre, 7-year old hay field that was 60% grass and 40% alfalfa located on a gentle slope. The irrigation ditch ran along the top of the slope so gravity carried the water down the hill. I split the 100 acres in to 15 paddocks of about 6 ½ acres each. The irrigation system was set up so one paddock could be irrigated at a time plus there was a ditch for drinking water.

The grazing cell was connected to a dry lot and a set of corrals.

The source and the type of cattle you run depend on the market and availability. When running steers, you don't want to buy someone else's fat. You want to put your own pounds on them. One year, I partnered with Buck and went to the Mexican border in February and bought 600 steers. Buck brought a crew down and we spent a week branding. When you own the cattle, you get to do it correctly. I haven't been to a good branding since.

We rented pasture in Arizona and I spent the winter with the cattle. In Arizona, they didn't gain much weight and we didn't want them to because we didn't want to ship more pounds than necessary. I shipped the cattle to Wyoming on May 15th and put them on my grazing cell.

The grazing cell rotation went like this:

Starting in Paddock #1, I grazed 600 head for 3 days. Then I moved the cattle to Paddock #2 and irrigated Paddock #1. I continued moving the cattle every 3 days and irrigating behind them as I went. By the time I had crossed the cell (grazed in each subsequent paddock for 3 days with 600 head), Paddock #1 had had a 42 day rest.

In June, we cut the herd in half and trailed the heavy end to Buck's ranch and turned them out. The balance spent the summer on the grazing cell.

We bought 400 wt. steers in February and sold 860 wt. steers in the middle of October. This venture happened about 15 years ago. It paid off well for Buck and me.

This type of ranching is typically done with a 4-wheeler. Instead of falling to those depths, I bought a bunch of horses and made them on the grazing cell. In the fall, I had a horse sale: Just another example of ways to make a profit on a ranch. I've never heard of used 4-wheeler sales turning much of a profit.

Before taking on a project like this, I sit down at the kitchen table with a piece of paper and a pencil and do the math. If the profit margin is too narrow, I don't do it. At that point, the only thing I've lost is a little bit of time. In the "Mexican Steer on the Arizona Border" scenario, the points I considered were:

- The number of steers we could run in Wyoming
- Purchase price
- Cost of Arizona pasture

- Cost to ship to Arizona pasture
- Death Loss
- Overhead in Arizona
- Freight to Wyoming
- Wages for Irrigator
- Overhead
- Freight to Market

Before jumping in to Intensive Grazing, I recommend going to Stan Parson's "Ranching for Profit School."

A yearling outfit operates at a faster pace than a cow outfit. After 30 years of experience, I've found that I like them both.

I'm sure you've figured out by now that a riding job on a ranch is a great way to enjoy life and a tough way to make a living. When you look at the ranching industry as a whole, you'll see that cowboys who do their job from the back of a horse only make up about 1% of the work force. But if I had it to do all over again, I wouldn't have it any other way.

One final piece of advice and I'll quit: If you want a wife (or husband!) to share your life with you, pick that person carefully. Don't marry someone who has to live on your dream. It has to be an equal partnership.

Miscellaneous Pearls of Wisdom to Help You Along

Here is a list of cowboy skills that compliment the ranch:

- Math
- Start Colts
- Make a good horse
- Rope
- Shoe
- Pack
- Build fence
- Cook
- Respect equipment
- Understand the reproductive system, digestive system, respiratory system, and endocrine system of a cow
- Understand gestation and the birthing process
- Deliver calves and understand malpresentations

- C-sections
- Preg testing
- Recognize diseases such as foot rot, scours, pneumonia, pink eye, anaplasmosis, forage poisoning
- Injections: IV, IM, SubQ, IP
- Simple operations such as removing kidney stones (water belly) and cancer eye
- Know how to read sign and track cattle
- Understand how to handle cattle
- Understand forage
- Learn about the sigmoid curve of grass
- Know the different grazing programs – rotational, intensive, deferred, open

Ranch Management Options

Lease bulls

Breed first calf heifers to a low birth-weight bull (goal: 50 lb calf at birth)

Have a 45-day breed up on heifers

Wean first-calf heifers at 110 days

Age brand all replacement heifers

Run yearlings

Sell hay

Winter outside cows

Implement an intensive grazing cell.

Run a band of sheep in addition to your cattle operation.

Have an annual horse sale.

Save a few thousand dollars on shipping day by already having your heifer pairs sorted from your steer pairs.

Be good at being simple.

Education

Stan Parson's "Ranching for Profit" School

Bud Williams' Livestock Handling School

Priceless Quotes

"Remember the best, cheapest feed you'll ever buy is good water."

"If you want to be a good cowboy, all you have to do is catch 'em in bed."

"If a cow is burning more energy than she is producing, you're going backwards."

"If you are burning more energy than you are producing, you're going backwards."

Yearlings at Rancho La Mentada, La Mission, Baja California (Courtesy of Enrique Loperena)

Castrating bull calves, Rancho La Mentada (Courtesy of Enrique Loperena)

Turning out at Rancho La Mentada (Courtesy of Enrique Loperena)

Branding Longhorn cows near Janesville CA

Feeding with a team and a few friends near Sierraville CA

Dragging logs out of the woods for a new barn, near Sierraville CA

Our niece, Brit, loaded and ready to go.

Heifers on the feed ground, RO Ranch, Big Smoky Valley, Nevada

Triple A Towing; taking a leppy calf home in a lick tub, near St David AZ

Tyler Vineyard, PK Ranch, Sheridan WY

Headin' home, Ventura County CA (Courtesy of Patti Martin)

Brandin' near Cuyama CA

Doctorin' at the RO

Made in the USA
Las Vegas, NV
08 September 2022

54939729R00049